Signed

AF251676

peter wild
NEW AND SELECTED POEMS

PETER WILD

NEW AND SELECTED POEMS

drawings by

DEBORAH EDDY

introduction by

WILLIAM MATTHEWS

NEW RIVERS PRESS
1973

copyright © 1973 by peter wild and deborah eddy
all rights reserved
library of congress catalog card number: 72-96038
isbn   0-912284-39-0 (cloth)
          0-912284-40-4 (paper)

ACKNOWLEDGEMENTS:
Thanks to the editors and publishers of the following magazines for permission
to reprint here the previously uncollected poems in this volume:
ANN ARBOR REVIEW, BELOIT POETRY JOURNAL, CAROLINA QUARTERLY,
DESCANT, EPOCH, THE FAR POINT, FOXFIRE, LILLABULERO, NORTH
AMERICAN REVIEW, PUERTO DEL SOL, THE TEXAS OBSERVER, THE
UNIVERSITY OF WINDSOR REVIEW, and WISCONSIN REVIEW.

Thanks also to the publishers of the following books and chapbooks for permission to use the material reprinted here:
THE AFTERNOON IN DISMAY, Art Association of Cincinnati, 1968
SONNETS, Cranium Press, 1967
MICA MOUNTAIN POEMS, Lillabulero Poetry Pamphlet #5, 1968
LOVE POEMS, Lillabulero Poetry Pamphlet #10, 1969
FAT MAN POEMS, Hellric Publications, Chapbook #4, 1970
TERMS & RENEWALS, Twowindows Press, 1970
DILEMMA: Back Door Press, 1971
WILD'S MAGICAL BOOK OF CRANIAL EFFUSIONS, The Little Magazine/
     New Rivers Press, 1971
GRACE, Chapbook #1, The Stone Press, 1971
PELIGROS, Ithaca House, 1971

new rivers books are distributed in england by:
          philip spender
          69 randolph avenue
          london, w9, england

in the u.s. and elsewhere by:
          serendipity books
          1790 shattuck avenue
          berkeley, california
          94709

this book was manufactured in the united states for NEW RIVERS PRESS,
p.o. box 578, cathedral station, new york, n.y. 10025 in a first edition of 1300
copies of which 1000 have been bound in paper, 300 in cloth of which 30 have
been signed and numbered by the author and the artist. .

FOR SILVIA

CONTENTS

AN INTRODUCTION

That Peter Wild's poems are many— there have been eleven books and pamphlets since 1967, ten of them represented here— is only the numerical expression of the profusion of his imagination. In one poem he is describing a curse.

> It travels, lightning branching
> through the soil,
> shoes plowing underground,
> a blind snake, roots, a pig nosing
> under rivers, deserts . . . .

The switch from the singular "it" to the plural "shoes" and "roots" follows quite naturally from the curse's first behavior, "branching," spreading as curses and gossip do. Also it embodies an energy I love in Peter Wild's poems. His mind moves this way, too, branching, jumping from one perception to the next. I sense in his terse style, full of apposites and end-linked constructions, the speed of a mind travelling fast on its own energies and the speed of someone hurrying to get it all in. The effect is of a baroque telegram, or the wildest photo caption you'll ever read. One poem starts like this:

> Farmer making hay defends
> his virgin daughter against the sun, who
> came riding his bicycle obliquely out of
> the white sky, nose to bar, lean
> arms and leather legs, grinning with his even
> false teeth like a fox pursuing a rabbit . . .

There are twenty-five more lines before the episode, the sentence and the poem end simultaneously. The poem never loses its full-tilt pace and zaniness, but its parody of a travelling salesman joke as filmed by Hollywood turns inside out. At poem's end

> in her empty
> lap landed a string of pearls, his teeth,
> which burned her hand
> in delight.

Other poems end mysteriously. In one a virgin comes through a Southwestern village selling eggs, "ringing a branch of bells, her breasts exposed. . . ." Yet in the next stanza she is "in peaked hat/ and thick glasses/ looking like a teacher" to the children who buy the eggs. That night there is rain and little snakes break out of the leathery eggs.

Much of the mystery in Wild's poems is native to the Southwest, where Anglo, Indian and Mexican influences mingle, and where the landscape that looks sparse to an easterner is thick with spirits, jokes, sudden malevolences. In Wild's poems there is none of the self-conscious exoticism of most regionally influenced poetry. The currently fashionable mode of bad Southwestern poetry is written by university-educated white rationalists who talk loudly about mystery and shamans, all the while explaining fully the spiritual mysteries of cultures now reduced by the poet's ancestors to the formulaic reproduction of tribal artifacts for tourist dollars. A sophisticated version of the same trade is offered visiting anthropologists and poets. But Wild is comfortable with whatever mysteries his region holds, even when they don't unravel themselves for his literary use. And he has a lovingly ironic sense of how regional clichés lie and reveal truth, both, about the land. The tact of a poem like "Variation *(cantelo con tristeza)*" is in this sense a spiritual achievement.

When his imaginative fecundity clashes, benignly, with his tact— when his love of invention and play lean against the resistant solidity of the physical world and his love for it— he writes very beautiful poems (from many, I'd pick "Vision in the Ceiba Tree" as an example), poems rich with perceptions that conflict in logic but not in our emotional lives.

In another of Wild's poems "wagons rumble by/ bearing away the dead, sitting upright." The same poem ends, "you can hardly speak in sentences." Not all the stutters in his poems, the tense sentences broken into chunks, are the record of a mind at happy play, that most serious of endeavors. There are in these poems not only lines, but also echoes and silences, which hold great terror. When the spirits and magical animals Wild loves retreat from the landscape, vast distances are seen to have been there always.

standing in a bowl
the edges tilt up, lost
across the middle of yourself;
and always ahead, a hint of peaks and waves,
            the liquid lies of mountains
      which you know, getting there, are scars and rifts
                  formed drip by drip,
            as if it will take you
            that long.

The poem sails along the margin for seven lines (I haven't quoted the first four) and then sets out for the white space of the page. Its ironic turn at the end is, for me, very exact. You will not get very far back, it seems to be saying, and also: you wanted to be here, and this is why.

For some time I've hoped for a book that would collect the poems Wild considers best from his early books and pamphlets, many of them now out of print. This New Rivers selection not only fulfills that wish, a wish shared by many readers, but includes some uncollected early poems and some new ones.

America's poetry economy is as inflated as her defense economy. The market is glutted with products that fall apart quickly. Even so, outrageous claims are made for them. Interestingly enough, little magazines and small presses, supposedly organs of resistance to literary piety, are the loudest proclaimers of this parish-level Renaissance. Good young poets will ignore this Rotarian clamor. They will be grousing over their poems, hoping to write better.

In this book, out of the bibliographical· traffic jam of his earliest publications, Wild's best poems gather. They are happy in each other's company. They are obviously the work of a man who wants above any other literary ambition to write good poems, and who can. It is a delight to read such a book.

— William Matthews

I

THE AFTERNOON IN DISMAY

Art Association of Cincinnati, Inc.
(1968)

CONSUELO OF THE MOON

Consuelo
carries green melons
beneath the cold moon.
the crickets in her hair
the serpent at her feet

she walks across
the newly-plowed earth,
the snow on the mountains
is hardly breathing:
from underneath the stones
beetles watch her
with huge eyes,
and in their nests
the birds talk in their sleep
as they dream

the snowfrost hangs low
in the contours of the earth
and her breath
turns to little puffs of frost

Consuelo carries
green melons.
the snake slithers quietly
into the brook
and the crickets
are nuggets of gold

she carries
green melons
across the newly-plowed earth.

THE MARVELOUS DOG

Across the steppes
comes the dog full of holes

in his mouth he carries
a salami sandwich;
on his head he wears
a crown of white onions

in the pouch around his shoulder
is a flask of clear vinegar

he is carrying in it
messages for his lady

to put on her face
to put on her hands.

he sees the sharp stars
moveless above him,
even now the
cherries burn in his eyes

as he runs with dusty paws,
smiling, and running faster. . .

he is bringing
messages for his glass lady
of clear vinegar

to put on her face
to put on her hands

and onions
to put in her eyes.

EL PEZ DE LA NOCHE

The fish of the night
carries a yellow lantern in his mouth.
his tail is made of a sickle.
his stomach is full
of sleeping men and women

he floats down alleys
and the rabbits kick in their dreams,
he glides down the street
and bumps his nose against the windows:

the fish of the night
wears a joker's cap hung with tin bells
and a fat monk's belt around his girth.
he lifts a leg to pee on the corner of a building:
and waking in the middle of the night
you can smell his stale breath as he passes
in search of fenders and empty bottles.

BROWN MOON

A brown moon rides upon the gulf
and a vast bay horse slips off the mountains
to paw the grass and feed on his reflection.

the distended city shivers in its bones
along the shore, rattles its teeth;
                              with pretty fingers
girls pull shawls over naked shoulders.

she rises tall from the distance of receding
plateaus, covered with burlap and dun armor.
oiled wheels turn slowly in her.

spoons sift water. the boat pivots slowly,
                              caught
in the field of a refracted promontory.
a herd of cartilaginous horses skitters on the plain.

luna lunera, díle que tenga compasión.

COLIMA

Suddenly
she jumped out before me
from behind a potter's stall
and ripped open her dress

on her breast lay
            a glass pendant
writhing in the sun like a snake.

and in it I saw
            a long path
lined with cool dark trees,
and fires burning
                far out on the ocean;
and heard the waves
                like happy soldiers
stumbling onto the shore

she was gone.
around me the peasants
            were still bickering,
and the sun cut into my head.

POEM OF THE VIRGIN SELLING EGGS

She came through the village
                on a Sunday,
barefoot and jeweled,
        selling eggs,
ringing a branch of bells,
her breasts exposed. . .

she came to the village
        from over the campos.
in peaked hat
            and thick glasses
looking like a teacher.

and smiling like a nun
                sold eggs
to the children.
            went away
down rows of dusty tamarisks. . .

we marveled
        that night
at the rain;
        and the little snakes
that broke out of the leathery eggs.

AN APOLOGY FOR WOLVES

I.

They have always
vilified us,
sensing our stealth
and their lack of it,

and moved by the first impulse
of their dim minds,
throw stones, beat shields,
catch us in their iron sights. . .

as if we wanted their women
or would steal their Gods. . .

II.

it is true, we've been caught
on occasion with the remnants
of petticoats still in our mouths,
or sporting a red cap, just for a lark.

but we've got a bad press
which capitalizes on such exceptions:
a grandmother or two
coughed up now and then,

and doesn't consider
our loss of face
when driven into the suburbs
by a long winter and heavy snows.

III.

actually, it's just a simple lack
of understanding—on their part,
a myopia common
to all muscular animals. . .

we mean no harm
but must pursue
that fine exhilaration
instinctively ours:

flaming tails in bushes
and leaves slipping along our backs.

TONGUES

The wind blows through the window
and fills the room,
freshens the bowl of flowers;
the sun glances on the deep varnish
of the furniture, strikes
the white sheets of the bed

shirtless,
I stand at the window
watching the city oxidize,
still and pink between
the quiet river and the sky;
as if perhaps in a hundred years
it will grow a tongue
and speak the words
to be remembered forever as holy:

you lie on the bed,
covers thrown back,
half stirred by light and wind;
also waiting for the kiss
to break you into day,

in your small mouth the tongue
struggles again and again
to form words which have no vowels
except those given by sunlight and wind.

SINGING PRINCE

Here I sit on my mat
before a basket of colored eggs,
playing my mandolin,
naked except for a crown

here surrounded by sand
and the stark walls of a blue sky,
I play, mindless of faces
which appear in the creosote.

I feel the wind on my ribs,
the sun on my stubble;
the sky is filled with yellow birds
and a fox comes, wagging his tail. . .

and at night when the mountains sink,
I stretch out, head on arm,
and sleep the dreams of ice cold water
sealed in ancient pottery.

THE ANGELS OF SAN SIMON

The angels of San Simon
        stand still as gas pumps
and leave no footprints in the sand;
leaning against the houses,
        all week long
they clean their nails
        or squint, slouching, out across the chaparral,
        gnawing their fingers to the bone;
the clapboards of the town
        are scrawled with their faint images.

for diversion
        they stir the dust
        into housewives' milk,

or unseen by cats
        delve into apple barrels
        and pit the skins;

with thin hands
        they squeeze the cowboys
        by their testicles.

they touch the yellow cows
        and bring the ague
        and fever in. . .

and on Sunday afternoons fly out
        to the stagnant air pooled
above the mountains, blowing their paper
horns into the stifled sky,
            etching oxidized horizons
with the brittle streamers
      of their fine wasted hair;

      making the rounds
              circle back
and land, scarcely breathing,
            and stand still
as gas pumps,
      leaving hardly a footprint
in the sand.

THE PALACE AT 4 A.M.

Mother,
    I am going home.

through the great transparent
                           ear
    hanging
        tense in darkness.

overhead
    an antediluvian bird
        with hollow bones
     (made for flutes)
    rakes the sky
        with its teeth.

my heart is made of an apple
        instantly full-blown
    and ready to be cut:
I have watched
  the digital afternoons
     blow away
      like pieces of smouldering straw
    into an amputated sky,
        which ignores them . . .

I want my bath now,
    of raw ambergris
    and charred cloves.

and stroke my sister's chilly backbone,
         picked clean of meat,
    while I watch them take her head away
    in a basket of brown roses.

in the roofless attic
        an antediluvian bird
                rakes the stars,
        like plankton,
                through its teeth.

Mother, I want to be born.

and a massive hound
        bearing a stomach of coals in his mouth
                knocks on the door
        with his wooden head.

II

SONNETS

Cranium Press
(1967)

Wooden tongues do not eat up my silence,
this night shot smooth with bolts, and a yard
of unchained dogs; goats sleep,
and all around the village stout bars
thump into place behind heavy doors.
the moon wobbles over the haystacks
like a virgin boy into a wilderness franchise:
my cabbage mind sprouts leaves of silver.

peg-legged old man, pass by, freeze—
wander drunken into the forest where wolves
will make you human in their bowels. but
at the corner I hear his clapper, the moist cough:
bolts twist in the buckling jamb,
dogs nibble on slices of the moon.

V RAM

Insistent pain behind the eyes announces
the turning solstice, the coming of spring;
gambit for marbles, season of weddings:
time for exams. my sinuses protest
the marching of the Ram, too slow the body
swings listless; marble muscles
cry repose, while a fermented grain
tears and grumbles in the dozing bowels.

but the good will know in their veins the time
to move for the proof of their ethic; the bad
flounder with broken forelegs in the receding
riptide of their dreams. I straddle the fence,
see dying moths in an old man's eyes, squirming
hooks of sperm in the genitals of a sleeping youth.

X MOON

On huge bony feet the moon
clatters over the horizon.

sleeping girls turn to stone,
arms of sleeping men to dough.

dogs in chains slip to mounds of snow,
birds tumble in their dreams;

and where he touches my sleeping skull
frozen grass grows . . .

corpses roll in their graves
to watch him pass.

he gathers all the white lambs to his bosom,
and ringing his tongueless bell twice

goes away, stepping quickly
over the black cats of the mountains.

III

MISCELLANEOUS UNCOLLECTED POEMS
(1967)

VARIATION
(cántelo con tristeza)

across the alley from the alamo
       live an old paint pony
   and a Navajo,
whose head is like a lump
      of black chewing gum;
  the horse
    has never brushed his teeth.

they stand there giving an Indian
    "howdy" to all that pass by,
a grunt, looking at the sky;
   the horse chews on the Indian's shoulder . . .

they used to wash their frijoles
       in the creek
   and pick their teeth around the fire;
get a little drunk once a week —
  until one day, looking at the sky
     they went away
down the railroad track,
    wishing, not looking:
toot, toot, they never came back.

KITE MAN

We first met our next-door neighbor
          rounding the corner of his house
                    with a kite;
he smiled and nodded,
          blurted his name,
but it trailed off in the
          wind as he ran. . .

beyond that we've never met him,
          but have become used
to his flashing by the windows
          with his kite,
his feet thumping across the wet lawns
     at night;

he appears an amiable man, sweatered,
                    standing far off in the fields
                    watching his kite
soar and dip in the spring winds;
and once by chance
          I saw it hanging
magnified against the eye of the moon. . .

occasionally we see his family
          staring from the window,
his children sunken-eyed
     and his wife's fingers white
                    upon the sill;
          I've called to him,
but he only nods and smiles,
          floundering through drifts, tugging
                    the icy kite,
looking back over his shoulder as he runs,
                    lips and fingers turning blue. . . .

FARMER MAKING HAY DEFENDS
HIS VIRGIN DAUGHTER AGAINST THE SUN

Farmer making hay defends
his virgin daughter against the sun, who
came riding his bicycle obliquely out of
the white sky, nose to bar, lean
arms and leather legs, grinning with his even
false teeth like a fox pursuing a rabbit

and he, turning sweat to bread, pricked
in the corner of the eye, saw his fall
swift as the stone shadow of an eagle and
reared back knotting his worn guts
and loins into a catapult; and she
sitting in the midst of the harvest like
her mother, cool flesh, legs tucked under
her, reading a book and amusing her puppy,
holy pendant lying on her untouched
                    breast

and knocked him down
            in the side of the ear
with one blow of his rake
    tumbling him sprawling hopeless from his
bicycle crushing the soft rims
                of his gold spectacles
his jaw flew off like a small pistol
                crack;
and he hit the ground like a pile
            of bones
                    and sank leaving only
a greasy pool on the earth

while she unknown in her empty
lap landed a string of pearls, his teeth,
which burned her hand
                in delight.

PICTURE OF THE COWS FEEDING ON MY HEART
(Irvine, 1967)

Here there is no daylight;
           a canvas tarp
        thick as a mountain range
oppresses the sky,
      lit by a lavender clock
           the face of a woman,
      hung with camel's bells. . .

the moon comes
        wearing a black armband
adolescent
         wound in moss bandages,
an old sea captain
      walking with a bone cane
    leading a kicking flour
         and water calf
    by a string

their black beards
      drag along the ground,
as they furrow the frozen earth
       turn up gold coins
           trample them
    in the dung,
in a barren place
     root up green skulls. . .

from the bitter night
  a sheep's head
     wrapped in a blanket
falls into my arms.

IV

MICA MOUNTAIN POEMS

Lillabulero Press
(1968)

RATTLESNAKE

We killed him with heavy rocks,
clawing them out of the dirt
            with the tips of our fingers,
frantic and red-faced in the heat,
throwing them badly, worse
                        than boys;
until we used the heaviest ones,
    compensating for our aim
            by weight and numbers,
and, finally, crushed his head . . .

I remember how he was crossing the road,
    in a straight line, fat with a mouse, and
                fourteen rattles,
but at the first blow
        made an instant stand to die;
how his excellent body
        hammered up, breaking his mouth
on the boulders we threw . . .

and how he fought,
        blind, broken
open in three places,
        head bitterly erect,
until we smashed his brain
    and he died twitching,
                slow as the stub of a candle . . .

and even then
        we were afraid to touch him,
he was so potent . . .

and drove away in our cars.

INDIAN PIPES

When the pastures and forests
            were smoking after rain
on an early spring evening
            we'd walk through the grass
wet up to our knees;
            already in the half dull light
                    the mists lifting
against the mountains
            and curling around the trees—
stoop through the heavy grass
            cutting Indian pipes;
        and walk, my father with the shaking bunch
down the brook
            under the dripping pines,
along the warm pond
    to the cemetery
            between its two Civil War cannons;
and be back, surrounded by frogs,
    just as the house got dark.

FLIGHT (I)

Learning how fragile life is
        easily crushed
or punctured
            letting the life-air out;
the bones not really living bone
            but more like plaster structure
the skin a thin cover
        stretched over cavities
                        and juices,
the whirling essential molecules . . .

just a hole
        a pinpoint smaller
than the smallest thought
                    or light
and they fly out
    the chest collapses;

sometimes lying in the darkness
            I feel the birds
            about to rush up my throat.

ROACHES

Last night when I got up
to let the dog out I spied
a cockroach in the bathroom
crouched flat on the cool
   porcelain,
    delicate
antennae probing the toothpaste cap
 and feasting himself on a gob
   of it in the bowl:
I killed him with one unprofessional
   blow,
scattering arms and legs
 and half his body in the sink . . .

I would have no truck with roaches,
crouched like lions in the ledges of sewers
their black eyes in the darkness
   alert for tasty slime,
breeding quickly and without design,
laboring up drainpipes through filth
   to the light;
I read once they are among
 the most antediluvian of creatures,
surviving everything,
 and in more primitive times
thrived to the size of your hand . . .

yet when sinking asleep
 or craning at the stars,
I can feel their light feet
 probing in my veins,
their whiskers nibbling
 the insides of my toes;
and neck arched,
 feel their patient scrambling
up the dark tubes of my throat.

DEATH OF A CAT ON RT. 84

Wounded in the middle of the road
she clung to the warm pavement,
biting her tongue,
       the icy stars
eating into the back of her head.
at 4 A.M.
     the cold black vacuum
of the desert
         moving alongside me,
windshield smeared with the guts
     of mayflies and spots of rain,
the black road standing still;
I clobbered her
      at sixty-five miles an hour
seeing her, too quick,
  a wind-blown rag
       near the center line,
she struggling up into the light
      to heal her broken flesh
and didn't jar the wheel.
the desert, cold and black,
   moved along with me,
beyond the Galiuros
     the night enflamed with lightning.

FLIGHT (II)

I awoke this morning my jaw
                    somewhat out of joint
and aching
            as I ground
        bananas
                and corn flakes;
through the bay windows drizzle fell
                    in the grapes.

outside the kitchen door
    three musicians stood stoop shouldered
                    in the rain,
waiting;
        knocking out my charred pipe
                I kicked aside a chair
and sprinted across the muddy yard
        to the coughing biplane;

snatching their burlap satchel
                of lavender edged letters
I buckled on my tight leather cap
        and forcing the throttle
splashed over the chuckholes,
        avoiding the cows,
into the striated sky,
    headed for the saddle between the peaks
smothered in clouds.

V

LOVE POEMS

Lillabulero Press
(1969)

SILENCIO

Your quiet,
        a semblance of mountains,
of cold peaks
                rising in the midnight air;
the quiet of mountain valleys
stirring darkly with coyotes and birds.

a desert stillness
            of quivering sand
and cactus rigid in starlight . . .

your silence
        the silence of water
in rock pools,
of water running over ledges
        in the darkness of unknown canyons;
black between moss banks
        and swirling smoothly around thick roots . . .

the moon comes
    and hangs on an ironwood tree,
like a butterfly come to rest,
    like a night flower in bloom;
and looks down
        with its bland oval face,
                and blows away . . .

your quiet,
        the quiet of boulders,
blackest before dawn,
and the long quiet of pale starlight
            in mountain pools:
when the birds shake their heads
                in the thickets

and morning comes, cool water
            in the canyons,
while the moon stares
            like a sick child
                in the evanescent sky,
the shattered desert
                tilts into sunlight,
and the brown hills
                and your brown arms
                            move
                into day.

MACIZA

In my arms
you are a whale
bursting through
            seas of flowers

from far off
I have seen the frothy
rock hills piling
            into mountains,

lost myself in their canyons
of smouldering piñon;
put my hand against
            the warm granite cliffs

and felt you there . . . .

DOLOR

You could not hold a pebble
without fearing
the curve of the earth,
shadows of pines
touched your heart
and it twisted in the flesh . . .

you understood
only as rocks became fire,
water turned to steam—

the earth pained
the soles of your feet;

you denounced the sun
for not sinking
to your darkness.

you hefted your life
like a broken arm.

VI

FAT MAN POEMS

Hellric Publications
(1970)

PARACHUTE FARM

Struggling to shore
   through the pink surf
we finally breathed,
     cut in every place,
  toes ragged from rocks,

bound our arms,
  oiled our swords;
viewed across the marshes
   a wild continent
  so flat the eyes went dim
a barn,
    upright mammoth cylinder

and rapping on the door
   it opened,
         saw
  the parachutes,
    silver,
   smooth as deer's thighs

crocodiles,
    wolverines
hunched
    on their backs,
  riding up and down
     on strings.

SOLDIERS

The soldiers waited
            by the bridge
        their Tommy guns
            pointed to the ground,
beards
     dripping in the water

an Indian canoe
        shot through the shoals.

I could see the spiders
        and maps,
            the love letters
protruding from their uniforms. . .

they raised their guns
        and sprayed the angels,
        bellies turgid with water
floating through the sky . . .

they ate our bananas
                and toys,
        one kissed my rosary,
     and let the bus pass.

ELK TOOTH

In my plexus
            an elk's tooth
      lies embedded

around it fester
      cuttlebones
                  shells
beaks

and other things
                  not easily
      digested.

sometimes it hurts when I breathe

sometimes convulsing
            I cough up
      tin cans, broken wrist—
bands, the foot
            of a crow

and at others
                  something hard,
      white
                  waxy,
      sweet, like ambergris.

POEM

I

He had an arm twelve feet long
        sometimes he would hear them
                calling him over the hill of the sea,
chorus of hair
        body of warm wind. . .

he would feel his chest
        when the palms moved
                like shadows of spiders and leaves
moving over beds of rock
        the center of noon
                tasteless on his tongue.

the cold sea foam covered his toes:

II

he had a red eye
        and the indolent hump of a mule
                at the back of his head;
he saw the seabirds
        rising white on the land wind.

at times fishhooks caught fire
        on his brow, and he saw bananas
                and smiling women floating
below him among the rocks;
        he spat

and the sea bristled white along the reefs.
    he heard the train pulling over the mountains
            he smelled the forest floor and hot pine boughs;
    he looked at his shoes:

he saw the seabirds
        rising on the land wind.

RESOLUTION

1.

Tuesday morning.
the gouged hardwood floors
        creak beneath my stockings.
the split bamboo curtains,
      sexless,
            offer no resistance,
but empty glasses, emerging vases
        things on my desk
      prepare to metamorphose
            like sleeping birds into snakes. . .
the cold mouth of the fireplace
        threatens to shout something obscene.

even up high
        where the sun is
the trees are coated with wax,
      nourished by corpses
        deep in the flaky alkaline soil;
a cardboard fish, with a filmy eye
            swims through the oleanders.

2.

at midday,
        when the soldiers
were sleeping in the plaza,
      bellies full of chili
            warm as tequila,
a shadow walked along the wall
            like a bruise,
like the reflection
        of a putrid cloud. . .

and rounding a corner
          met him face to face,
his cheeks shot away,
          revealing a head
    clustered with brittle honey;
lightning flashed in his eyes
      like moths,
his breath smelt
          of juniper berries. . .

3.

having eaten the heart
          out of mushrooms
the birds fly away;

I stand ankle deep
          a stalk of celery
stricken by axes.
the stars swim around me
          in the sullen water.
smoke is rising
          from the cedar trees;
a lusty coyote
      runs over the dry hills,
a chicken in his mouth. . .

          prayers of Indians
issue from the canyons;

    little sugar bells
          hang in the crevices
      of the night.

DRIVING TO WORK
    (Orange County)

Each day I mark
    how the freeways
       and orchards
have slipped toward the sea. . .
    the fields and their thousands
               of plants,
orderly as crosses. . .

further inland,
    how factories and municipal
buildings, their smokestacks bent,
  nudge through muck,
      battleships straining toward the ocean. . .

the streets are full of schoolgirls,
    naked and covered with sores,
stumbling like paraplegics
    down the sliding ramp of the suburbs. . .

pausing in his shackles
    a mule grins
and vomits a plethora
       of stars;
when I get home
    a black dog
      waits hungry in the yard,
weary astrologer,
    to plunge into my veins.

I feed the mouth of the lion
                candles
            tarantulas
                net the walls,
    rise in the dome;
                the snow blows in
                            beneath the door
                she screams in the wood,
    frozen feet twisted in the grain. . .
    a purple breast
                presses against the window. . .

I strike my forehead to the stone
                lay sweaty coins
                between his plaster toes—
    he leers down from the golden throne

and as I leave,
                mouth full
                    of plastic toys
        babies' arms
                    jeweled receptacles,
    he spits them out;
                    they bite my flesh
            like spiders,
                    like shattered glass. . .

ice grips my wrists
            I see his footprints
                    across the winter sun.

CHIRICAHUA HEAD

From his earlobes hang
        biplanes
                and locomotives,
      his eyes glow muddy and
                      red
at Orange Butte

early in the morning
        a giant grasshopper
sails over his mastoids;
        his thoughts still muddled
in a mouthful of sand;
      he sees the withered angels
              of San Simon
and feels the ruptured capillaries
         twitch in his groin;
horses, cows, deer
      go to bone before his eyes. . .

before him the colors
        slide along his lap;
 axletrees
   cobalt bottles,
tangles of rusted barbed wire
   he offers to the gods
       smouldering in his head;
and when it rains
     coughs up a demented cowboy
pale and brittle
      as a lizard. . .

across the great cow
            of the valley
      the mountains float like islands,
the doughy land
            folds on itself into cracks;
he counts the chambers
            of his pistols
      loaded with blanks
and spits through the hot wind
            at the droplets of lights;
sleepless through the lean night
            glows like a burning snag.

COMPENDIUM: FOR SOUTHERN CALIFORNIA

What matters is the distance,
        the space through the trees;
but here at eight o'clock
    the bodily functions
        echo from cubicle to cubicle.
daily the groves are shorn
    and buildings rise, teeth
  sown in the rut of the blade. . .

morning collapses, a stabbed
        deer on the threshold;
we struggle for our clothes,
    iron garments that allow some room
  against the public weal,
with our own blood and ashes
        cross our foreheads,
            enter the street. . .

here every gesture becomes
    a risk for the heart,
        an act of survival;
  we keep the chambers close:
    even in total darkness
        the roots eye the seasons,
the plants move their leaves up and down. . .

TWO GIRLS WALKING TO SCHOOL

Above them the stars swirl,
                shine on the clods;
    their shoes worm through the dirt.
lining the fields cottonwoods
        stand rigid, frosted,
    as the wind flaps their skirts,
    burns their knees;
a white moon perishes

their talk is like macaroni,
        like bubbles; it flies from
    their lips without a sound
  and circles the world,
falls through the trees,
    falls on the backs of mules;
before them the machinery roars. . .

as the wallpaper flames,
    heads big as pumpkins,
    they sail about the narrow room,
bumping the ceiling, scrape their shoes;
        hold their niño cristo, crepe
  roses, wan pictures of the lady
in rainbow. . . they float
                out the window
        over the snow

over stables with their steaming
        horses, over forests, over
  swimming pools — over spindly
ice palaces burning their hands
            white; they circle
  the world. hear the songs of
negroes. . .
        clutching rosaries on their bosoms
    they swim brown and dry
                    as paper roses,
      in seas of menudo. . .
until sucked
    into the tide of that ox, the moon. . . .

EL BURRITO

While I was riding home
        one day to my sandy ranch,
    a little bit fat and a little bit
    tipsy—Saturday still knocking
in my head.
                    I thought I heard a
    voice behind me, but the road
        was long and covered with thickets. . .

and crossing a wash—no birds
                    above me—yes, there
    it was again, and turning saw
    a little burro fawning, tacos
                    for eyes;—I said
        little burro go home this
is no place for you alone—the mice
            will get you. . .

threw a stone,
        paid no attention; but
    when I stopped again there
he was,
            silver tongue,
        biscuit breast—
                nuzzled to my chest,
                        said
            hee-haw hee-haw and jumped
        into my lap. . .

FAT MAN

He walks through seas of himself,
        always deeper; horizons fade

the water beats his chest,
        rushes in; rises warm to his chin.
    losing his shoes, his feet,
            bones separate,
    float. . .

muscles swim.
    mollusks, barnacles, weeds
        grow along his skin;
    flotsam, fishes,
        nuzzle in the folds. he draws
            his clustered world behind him;
    happily waves his arms,
            and the birds fly,
                then settle on his head. . .

becoming his own universe, he sits
            watching the far-off girls
        thin as beaten gold. . . .

ABOUT THE GRAPES

What they don't understand
        is because they haven't thought
    about the grapes,
            deeply enough,
    breathed them in. . .
or perhaps not at all
        but only heard
            the current propaganda
    dismissed or accepted
                while switching channels. . .
and even those who rave,
        their hunger rising red to the skin,
                understand nothing,
    have thought nothing,
        sense only the lack raving in themselves. . .
    but I have listened long,
            seen the grapes clustering the earth,
        seen them dense with rain,
clustering hill on hill,
        curls so tight
    that beneath the ground swayed mad with them. . .
no machines or men; but that they grow
        on moonlight, the unseen decomposing soil.
    and that at night only foxes
            and crocodiles
                    feed on them.

RAIN

When it rains
     the frogs sing;
   they climb out
from their holes
  and sit in the dry marshes
    on their dry haunches,
     eyes sparkling,
listening to it come. . .

they hold out their tongues
    and leap newborn,
red mouths flashing,
   as the storm washes
    the scales from their backs

and for nights after
   lie in the flooded ditches
like pieces of black rubber
    singing. . . .

VII

TERMS & RENEWALS

Twowindows Press
(1970)

ON A LINE BY CHEKHOV

The intentions are revealed.
    and the designs needle
        like thistles bunching in the blood.
    shall we choke in the skirts of angels. . .

once, abandoning ourselves to a land
    where the houses had fallen,
    the cattle ran wild through the thickets,
        bowels of virgins
           waving from their horns. . .
    the groundwind and dust
        filled our breeches.
on the fortieth day we saw a cloud,
    warrior's head thrown back
to the heavens; watched his pink slit jaw
    drift off down the range. . .
that night in the rain
        scratched our knees,
    waited for messages. . . .

INDIO

Naked boy, you lie stretched
among the withered palms,
tangled in scrap, tracks
around your neck; owls
eye you and at noon the
sand eats your thighs. numbed,
you watch those seven chanting sisters
circle, circle the horizon in their flimsy
skirts, holding your breath
as one about to be eaten. and
on holidays, unable to lift your
head, listen as dirty towheaded girls
hide in the washes preparing toasts
for your honor with cups of sperm. your hands
break out with asterisks, countersinks,
oil stains—a locomotive roars
through your head. . . even now
the peaks rise white, creamy with it,
while bones green, the burnt flesh falls
back from them; a pitted sun smiles
through your ribs.

CAMPERS

Laboring from the year,
uphill from the Great Plain of their lives

they drag their entrails with the weeks,
cicatrix love, their paraphernalia

finally the pines. as advertised. they groan,
the sun doesn't sting their faces; they don't

know why. and grunting at nightfall dig
the pit, line it with a bear's charred bones

polish his skull. it glows,
they titter. stretch out with weary beers

flabby legs to the lake, their footstool;
time to go in, to crank the shutters down.

satisfied, the rangers go home.
while perhaps, over the next hill, at the

bottom of the next undeveloped mountain
there are those few, perfectly alone, famished,

who roll up their jeans for a pillow.
stretching in ferns among the spiders throw

scrawny arms to the gloom, lie there
as the damp night crawls from the ravines,

mouths open, waiting for the stars
to eat their eyes.

SNAKES

The rattlesnakes have begun to come out,
                into the gardens,
        out of the mountains,
                from the parched fields,
        after water it is said,
                after mice;
the papers have announced it,
    we find warnings
                tacked to our doors—
I think one gardener,
                a faithful servant,
        has been bit, stooping
to tend a marigold,
                and a child reported
        her hand horribly mangled—
the citizens have been armed,
                mothers keep their
            brooms by the door,
                police carrying shotguns. . .
I have seen none. walking
        barefoot through the beds,
    checking the mulch
                behind lattices,
            even rabbit burrows. . .
I have never been harmed;
but last night fidgeting
        I awoke dizzy to sweet music;
outside on the lawn, the road,
    the housetops, our flowerbeds
                were full of them, almost erect,
their thin necks
        swaying toward the moon,
        humming, smiling,
                sensuously

drinking in the light;
while others sped
            back and forth on great
                rice-paper wings,
carrying messages
        across the cloudless night. . . .

TERMS AND RENEWALS

All at once everything
drawn to a circle
convulses; and the sun
lays its satin tongue in the grass.
but for that, we are thrown
backwards with the debris,
arms, legs, phonographs, giraffes,
thrown as light on water from
a dog's back; landing in weeds,
some limbs spread useless, others
tangled about the head, each foundering
in dung, beneath the old bland sun
lapping at him, rocking himself
in the arms of his own cradle; reach
out, reach in. grow again.
sneeze.
pluck the strings.
make harmony of that.

THE DAY THEY TOOK THE GOATS AWAY

At the scheduled hour I bleat
the secret bleat, but around the
peeling corner comes no answer;
puzzled, I stand out into the yard
with my shadow, before the open
gate, the empty pen, stricken
with a cabbage hanging from
each hand; they are gone. and the
sun strikes me down. and catch
in the tail of one eye the fat
owner, hairy elbow out the window
driving down the farm road puffing
his cigar. in a corner of the truck the
little one, who jumped through my
arms light as a rainbow, lies weeping,
a crushed fawn; and the mother, one eye
blackened, stretches a paw through the
tailgate, as they go waves
      good-bye, good-bye. . . .

FIREMAN

Look, the fireman has a pipe
in his mouth, turtles
sprout on his greasy vest.
he looks down the runway
of the hill to where the truck,
polished, red, stands mired
in the swamp, bellowing. . .

above him the harpies
are singing in the tower, their
black hair with the north
wind twining among the bells,
golden ropes and hoses. . .

on the mountains he sees a shiny
colt, and dreams of girls with
tawny haunches drinking water;
his nails are cracked. oh look,
a puppy lies
        dead by his feet with the stack
of greasy magazines. . .

            do not
pull the flower from his
coat, the pipe from his mouth,
or you will pull out his skull,
his vessels and viscera. . .

                from the clouds
they lean out and tickle his ears
with straws.

LAST NIGHT EMILY DICKINSON

Last night Emily Dickinson
        flew over my house
on a fried chicken liver,
            mushy grass hair
                    unloosed
and her apron
        tucked up
        under her white knees.

she went by teeth bared,
            digging her nails
    into the fried crust
        of the vitual,
as if to make it scream;
    cursing it in a
            language I could not
understand
    for fright.

goats rose up their curious heads
    all around the horizon
to see what had gone
            wrong with the world
(draped with damp seaweed
    like bridal veils,
some still with tin can lids
    or tough leather shoe tongues
            in their mouths),
and lolled. . .

she shot
    over the dark margin of the trees
like a comet
        bound to explode;
and in the pale light of it
    I saw their bloodless faces
    white like the heads of tapeworms
turn in an even sweep
        to watch her go. . .

we set our teeth
    but the explosion
        never came. . .
so we went back to bed;
there were only grease spots
        on the window panes. . .
    in the imminent darkness
    like a butterfly
        my heart tore
        in two.

TÍO

It would take someone like Tío, a real
hatchet man, ravenous as a gull, gull-
hearted, grinning against the lie
that his own grin supposed, to chase a tit,
raising the tortilla high like a cleaver,
shaking the house to make manners right;
he shouldered the table and over the steps,
the silhouette of a windmill behind the
five-year-old girl, who made herself
a chubby streak down the sidewalk,
her angel's wings, chicken bones begun
to flap, a glide across the ditch and
around the corner, already learned
to dodge—and twisting block around block,
finding holes through yards like a
rabbit, lost the jackal without a sense,
long ago quit, enamored of his wit, willing
to risk a joke for his loss; disciple of
vultures and Hoffa, dogs snarled
at his shadow, too lean to hold darkness
   or water.

and she sitting on a fencepost
labyrinths away thought about
the sun, watched the mating struggle
of two beetles on a leaf and much later
circled back when things had blown
over, replaced by other matters more easily
avoided.

MODEL

I

The wood is done with you
and now a bird thrown
all limbs broken heaped
in the midst of a centerless
plain, the asbestos afternoon. . .
no wolves howl beyond the
ridges, bones poking through,
cheekbones bruised by the sun.
ribbons unwrap from the legs like chains
coming loose, and the legs untie themselves,
walk around the body. your guano hair comes off
in patches, wanders over the skin
looking for a place to grow. . .
gaze down on the contours
of your flesh, exhibition
of knuckle bones, half moons, thumbs
pressed into the bone. . .
collapsed into the middle of your
peasant rags—one white breast noses
out, a worm, looking for a hole. . .

II

Because it is a beach and beneath the six suns
regular as soldiers.
your legs slide out, one
hand in the pocket of your thigh,
the world beneath an elbow. . .

breasts hard as chewing gum,
concealed in paper bags. and
covered just below the hips
on down. you view the boys
coming in, bobbing on the sea. your
hair takes root. eyes fill with
birds. the beach turns sky-blue
and they stumble through the surf
with bloody knees, tongues lapping up
the sand, as you point, and they squat
before their labor, chiseling moons
on your abdomen. the toes
dig in, and across your face
the lips, two strips of sky. . . .

THREE POEMS FOR THE GOOD YEAR BLIMP

I

You come out of the ears of a jack
    rabbit who sits on the
  hill sucking his thumb, taking
    soundings of the green-fruited
        afternoon; from between
  the singing cactus. . .
      all the rattlesnakes
  lunge to strike your belly,
to cling there like barnacles,
    the canvas of tennis shoes beatified,
      but flop back
  jangled, mad,
    teeth gone to charcoal. . .
and circle away over our afternoon
untouchable,
    quiet as an hourglass.

II

There is a buzzing in the ears,
    as from insects or minutes,
  the pollen of jungles,
    the pollen of the sea
      passing through our dreams;
one remembers the hog-nosed grouper,
    the fish with all their lights. . .
  the tadpole shaking off his skin
      to be something concrete, sunsets,
        mountains.
but you are drier than these
    and not so full of light,
  more like Bibles,
    the moth-gray ash of that
woman who fell from the tree
      toward a candle;

but no eyes. . .

you strip off our foreskins,
                 strip off our hats. . .

III

What do you see up there,
             circling the corrida,
      our bins. . .?
    maidens in back seats,
             maidens picking their
          golden hairs under trees. . .
  whole villages dancing
             through the festive labyrinth
    that empties over the sea.
priests in cells
             cracking their knuckles

you bob between the steeples.
    at suppertime you glide down
             alleys and peer into windows;
  smell the cabbage,
             see all that is going on there
                 like a map.
  you look into my heart
      and rise over the peaks
    on the rising heat,
             perhaps humming a private
    song of sacred monkeys and vines. . .
                 and are gone
             finding it tasteless.

98

INCIDENT

Dragged from the wagon before
the mules had stopped, the father
now a quick Jack and the boy
cortex dead slumped in his
arms. three blinks to the
house where they waited,
having heard his rattle, the lash
of reins thrown against the sun;
they put his leg in kerosene,
watched the green lye curl
where the tooth was, a
scum twisting to the top of the pail;
still watched the leg, the slumped boy,
its runners spreading across the floor,
testing the cracks, climbed the walls
until turning filled the
room with itself.

meanwhile the young doctor
arrived at this his first
case of nature, outside stood amazed at
foliage bulging the windows

and the father having gone
back where the foot
lurched through, dug
the mole's burrow, heard
fangs against the shovel;
struck. found another and another;
and probing the cavern saw
how it extended,
how it was full of them twined in
the tunnels, feeders, rooms; spreading
spreading palmately under the ground.

SCALLOP

On a mountaintop
        miles from the sea
we found a shell,
        and saw how the sea
had left the land
            rolled in waves.

this shell
        a million years old,
with the animal's skin
                dried to its back
        and bleached white as old cow bones

yet still the lustre, orient
            and pearl, caught in the flanges—
        the same that Venus rode on
                when she crossed the sea—
and in a corner the same pink
        as in the corner of your eyes. . . .

POEM FOR LEONARDO SÁNCHEZ

Where had the cock gone, the
golden one crowing himself away
above your garden, a frozen mist
dissolving to the drawn-out death
of many dawns. and but
for the old braves creeping out
with wooden rifles from the burnt-
over hamburger stand, and the white
slave girls kept as a burden, your village
was a two-hundred year old crepuscular
rose—the church dark enough to
swallow them, and the yard in front
for playing bolas. . . especially the
lads who had nailed themselves up to
display their sinews for the girls. you
came down the steps still emboldened
by the night before, and tucking your tail in.
it would take a new lift, a new aluminum
chair, and a thousand pounds of candy; drove
us around to those as had need. but the
pregnant women never stumbled from our arms
toward the fury of a demon, the church neither
gasped flame, nor sucked them in. he
eyed the corn on their breasts but remained
a stone on my ribs. Leonardo, the steps
of your house are rotting in, and though we
can lift your son, perhaps assuage
these children, they swing so far on
our intricate devices that soon the blood
your fathers tasted as pride and
musk of the wolf will be phlegm in your throat,
the streets where the girls roll full of prayers
and drunken, where we fornicate,
will no longer be grim.

FÉNICAS

Now the girls are driving home.
their thin breasts are resting,
                    loose balls of feathers
          against transparent ribs.
they hardly grip the wheel.

the roads out of town whip
    and then straighten. along curbs
  palm trees wilt, lash at the
          sunset, then yawn, tired lions

past churches where the Virgin
    laughs, points to her orient
  nipples, past houses
where bald husbands
        dash furniture against the walls.

behind them TV sets are coming
    on in the barrios; they pass farmers
  trudging home behind their teams;
the red sun pools on corn leaves

poinsettias bloom in their navels
        their breasts writhe against the windshield.
by the seats of their pants they feel
        the sunset roar

the whoredom of Malinche. . .
        and swinging into the drive
    the ravenous chickens
            rush out to meet them.

CABEZA DE VACA

What could they do at the sight
   of the man, thrashing, lunging through thickets,
   the head of a cow and bleeding
from every pore, but fall back astounded,
                sharpen their arrows. . .
from the reeds they watched him stop,
      clutch at his throat, stare into the sun
   and groan;
                birds pulled his hair,
   the rivers had no directions. . .
                some took him in
to ease the gods, sat amazed
      at his stupor, others peppered
the beast with arrows; but for him,
         truly beside himself, alone,
      there was no difference
   but to pull himself from thorn to thorn,
                            following
   the maid that lured him
         golden-shoed and blouse open,
                from horizon to horizon. . .
and at last, every night as the earth rose
      black with its calls to devour him,
   to lie back ready to be eaten,
         to bathe his tongue
   and slip into the mud. . . .

DOME ROCK MOUNTAINS

What we'd see stumbling
for weeks over those dry reefs
of mountains, stiff avalanches worse
than dungeons cutting our soles,
that rose and fell with the heat,
cataclysms where even the deer
ran in circles, starved and died
passing the dead mouth of the
La Posa mine, and further on
the miner weeps over his
cannibalized burro—for
months of continuous nights
beneath stars lashing us and blooming
coral pricking our eyes; finally, whirling
in loneliness, eating stones, gnawing
                              our belts
find the peaks needling up through
our hearts, and on the uppermost
a billy goat in nimbus braying
the gospel, one split foot on the
chest of a virgin, from which
                  all iris springs flow.. , .

VIII

DILEMMA: BEING AN ACCOUNT OF THE WIND THAT BLOWS THE SHIP OF THE TONGUE

Back Door
(1971)

MRS. WOLLER

The day after Mrs. Woller came home
            the cats returned to our back yard,
        climbing our elms, rolling through the weeds,
            giving our dog
                a bloody nose

so that day
        after her return from the Northwest,
            Skagway by the Passage, and lush California
I had to lay in
                a new pile of rocks

even before unpacking
        she had tottered off the kitchen porch,
shading her eyes,
    left a saucer; hearing it they
scrambled from caved sewers in the ravine,
        from stone foundations,
                dropping, it seemed, from the very trees . .

evenings I hiss and stamp,
        scan the bushes with my light
        before locking the shed,
                letting out the dog,
and wandering barefoot through the yard,
            listening to the trees roll,
                perhaps looking at the stars

see her by the lamp
        in her straw hat reading,
        cats perched atop her chimney
                tiptoeing across the roof,
        pacing up and down her veranda,
                looking in at her through the window. . . .

CANNAS

When I water the cannas
spiders jump from the straw
and climb over the house.
they crab up the stucco,
to the eaves, where they
squat . . . and
when I finish climb back
down, picking through the mulch
straw by straw to their
gauze homes, where they sit
in the oil-colored water,
looking out, perhaps
dreaming of this green world.

DILEMMA

The kid squat in a lawn-mower-driven go-cart
and helmet who has used the summer
                    skidding up and down the street
whom I've shot sheaves of arrows,
                              streams of
      bee-bees at to no effect,
                          bouncing off his smile,
        then bouncing off his back
                    finally has broken down.
            chin strap hanging
    he knocks at the door; I slam it in his face.
stands in front of my house over the thing
        tinkers awhile, then slides down beside a
                              wheel
      the sky pools in his eyes.
pretty soon the August sun begins to get him;
      I watch as oil drips from his fingers
    his skin turns black and shrivels,
                  ribs open.
the neighbor across the street, a retired soldier
          shows mercy by releasing his dogs;
  in a chain they clear the fence
                    before I can protest,
            tear him apart
            leaving only a grease spot
                  which they gather around to
                              lick.

ESPANTAR EL SUEÑO

The angel of sleep stands by our bed
          leaning on her black sword;
     our tongues rise from the graves of our mouths,
        fireflies, tips of waves that
       move across the darkness

the pictures hang silent.
        our feet are saints' feet,
arms dead moths.
still we cling to the dream,
     to go back and run through the tangled wood
   and never meet the house,
         holding hands, keep running . . .

the webs grow deeper on her,
     she shines;
  sighs, yawns from her armpits,
         her spider mouth.
   beneath the bed her heavy feet move. . . .

THE STORY OF DOLOROSA

Going to her knees every
time the fox circled back

a handful of flame, a bouquet
        between the knuckles

and further out the Indians
        coming in, cutting at his tendons.

every day thereafter she labored
        up the slope, rice sore in the skin

that madness for collecting wood. her
relatives would talk of other things

to have the smell of a sheep
                cradled in her armpits,
        the black tongue

 nightly the fire rose,
        she sucked it through her veil

behind her in darkness
        the village watched.

FOR THE EL PASO WEATHER BUREAU

In the heat of the day a funnel cloud
was sighted north of the Franklin Mountains.
out on their lawns seeing it move the residents
took off their guns, went to their knees;
touched fingertips to lips. closer
they saw how something like a sheik
sat in its middle playing a flute.
sparks shot from his head
and around him butterflies
on gold chains floated through the spirals.
they smelled burning flesh. in the gloom
some had roses spread like wounds over
foreheads
and chests, that dripped
a viscid liquid, clear sperm
on the ground. they prayed harder.
it never touched down.

VISION IN THE CEIBA TREE

When God made the world
he took a blue opal
and painted it with mud

and smoke.
on the hills he put bamboo groves.
there's where the cats lived
to fight with the angels

and the broad valleys
he paved with Bibles. also
in the greatest ones he planted stout forks,
like slingshots.

no one knows
what goes on underneath all this. except
some who have dug said the earth
tastes like sky

others have lain
for years with their ears to it
and went away shuddering.

and the houses, the
stone huts and white villas
he gave to the rabbits.

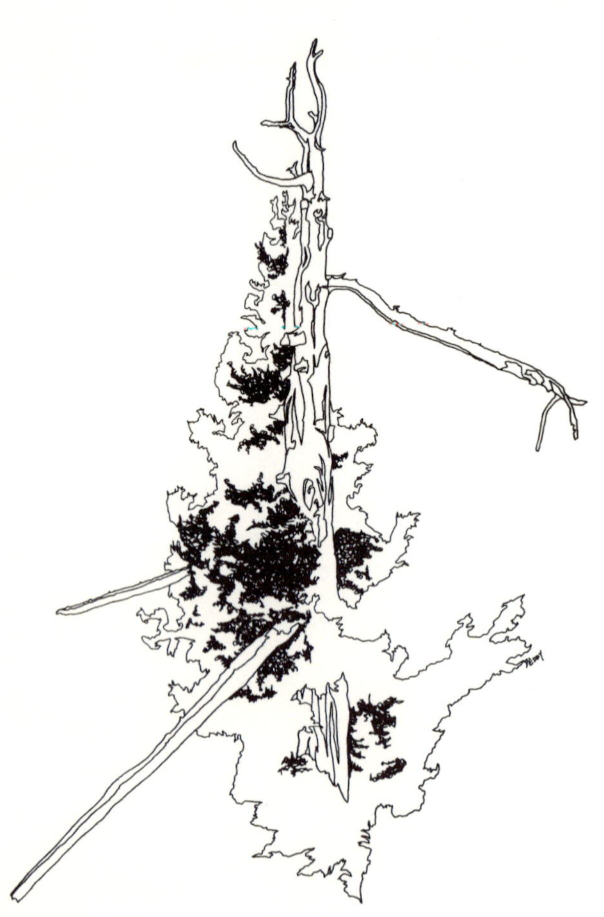

IX

WILD'S MAGICAL BOOK OF CRANIAL EFFUSIONS

The Little Magazine/New Rivers Press
(1971)

FOREST

The Chinese have been through the forest
in their pickups.
orchids stand among pine cones,
here and there rags tied to trees.
we follow their traces,
narrow tires over broken needles.
here a trunk is slashed with a Madonna in it;
a ravine, and beyond a cloud smothering a mountain.
we pick up spent cartridges, a hand
in a sleeve, a vial. the false teeth
begin to rattle in our pockets. it starts to rain.
frogs tumble from heaven.

THE BRIDE

I want to be forgiven for locking you in.
you float around, a burning fox
looking out the windows,
ironing shirts, thinking up poems,
barking.
while I am walking over cobbles
that are hot nails,
walking as a coalminer walks
up the hill where they meant to build a madhouse;
and coming home
find it strange seeing you beneath each plum tree
drinking wine, surrounded by angels.

MAN SLEEPING WITH HIS CHEEK IN THE SAND

Dawn blew away
one of his cheeks
so that he woke
looking into the hole
where his teeth had set roots . . .
                          he
closed his eyes and listened
to them pumping oil
through his skull, rushing
around the chambers where
by now on the inside flies
had gathered, bees
brought honey,
whole gardens flourished
and put out fountains, statues . . .
listened while the buzzing
drove a pyramid through his head,
as on the other side a soft
flap opened and the stars
whispered out. . . .

WUPATKI

If I were that elk
          smoking a cigar
     circling out
       a brandy in each hand,
    the land a film
          unwinding through my eyes.
       a lick of salt,
             nostrils split.
nosing even to where the escarpment came down,
          nosing the pines.
     going up through a forest
                    dry as moths' wings,
          setting fire to the pants of the settlers.
eventually to the topmost mountain
       burnt up, snowed on, soaked
          scooped out, looking in
       its throat filled with rainbows
                and gourds.

THE ONYX-EYED OBSERVER

He rubs his cigar butt out on the
sidewalk with his foot, like a dog turd

and walks away. preferring
intaglios, blonds, diamond rings

the genius behind airplane wings,
topographic surveys; any girl he has a number. . .

the fine hairs along the back of the Police Chief's wrist;
at noon disappears down wells

it is he you hear in the next stall in the washroom
counting to himself, coughing his lungs out

one foot on the head of the dawn; makes tricks,
bites the serpent's head off

with a wink; a handkerchief
floating on the evening. . . and who

lies in attics above where children
sleep, all night breathing. . . .

STORM

Yesterday a tornado struck
and did us in,
teeth impacted in teeth,
our jobs, manuscripts
spread around the neighborhood.
the main street bulged
then went to pot.
most of us stuck around
digging our claws into the soil
while elms whizzed by
streaming their roots, parts of garages;
but the dogs were whipped
into a handful, sucked
from alleys, from under beds;
they funneled over our house
howling as they rose into the cloud
that spun away toward the desert.
today the town was quiet
as we picked ourselves up;
the two streetwalkers smiled from doorways.
relief trucks arrived.
and by sundown they began
to trickle in, limping, shaking
their heads, mossy-eyed,
none the wiser. . . .

X

GRACE

The Stone Press
(1971)

GRACE

The diseased and the undernourished
are storing up thousands of hours of grace
by their distress

which is an extra set of planets,
                stars and soft-globed moons
buying time

rotting teeth in a rotten jaw
      held together by gold braces.

the deluded monk in his cell
        becoming childish,
      rice sinking into his knees,
   boats travelling through the sheet of blood,
our backdrop

a man sitting under a tree,
      talking to it;

the girl cutting her breasts
      bit by bit with razors

at sunset the red lion
      is seen walking over the backs of the palms
   grinning;
we hold up our hands momentarily to the sun
        and feel the liver cleansed

andwhat will we dare
      say to them,
   but hold up our hammers and saws
as armor
      as they lean to kiss us on the ear.

BEHIND THE ESTRELLAS MTNS.

It is cold so there are
few children. they play
anyway. you leave the park behind
and around the next few cinder hills,
past the Girl Scout Camp, get out.
the cactus stand there.
the gravel road flashes in your eyes.

at the sharp gulch cutting down through strata
no trace of bolts and timbers. you
scramble down then out. the
tracks stop, this is where your life begins.

like antique furniture, the ancient
hymns. old gold, a hand sticking from a rock,
cavalry cartridges. this is what you're looking for,
isn't it?

all around the granite mountains
sweep away and up in studded waves,
the sun on dry rock.
and dodging through the bean trees the moon
a wax basket with no one in it.

on the desert there is no middle ground.
things claw at your face or
whirl away; even the mountains,
standing in them.

SUCCESS

Each day you put on your makeup
with varying amounts of success
and get into the car.
it starts. the continuing miracle.

pencils write hardly
needing an agent. sharpened,
that is beautiful

the smell from the mulch pile
warm and sweet as flowers.

and give thanks to God
for the makeup and the car,
and the pencil,
but especially, for the mulch pile

and drive out to the wharf
where the waves are playing tricks
under the sun, and the oil slicks
race back and forth

as if you were trying to remember something
                                    unsaid,
as if your full name were just an initial.

GIRL WITH A COOKIE AT HER LIPS

It won't stay down
but comes rushing out dog bones
and lumps of gold that fall into heaps
of hearts and letters on the ground.
a sparrow sits on her mouth
spitting in kernels and peas
that make the sound of coins
dropping through a machine,
a warrior with a beard,
a giant grasshopper kissing her.
deep down the minute ice and
bladed words cut through the mud of her bowels.

ECLIPSE

On their stems
the stars lean,
wheat heads bent on the wind

snakes returning
to their nest, to bite
the cinder

out in the yard
you have come prepared,
new shoes and a new shirt
and body almost clean

but not for this.
the trees show their bones;
the crust gives beneath your feet.
it is real

as a picture. and closer
you lose control of your eyes,
your facial muscles. your arms
flap around in their sleeves.

Watch, the Indians have a hold on you
where they sliced at the rock with their arrows.
the moon is reaching
into your veins with its brown hands.
beetle browed
you look out over the creosote.
each step you take is a giant one.
when you lift a foot, it is in slow motion
and the plain follows, swaying up and down.
going over Bee Mtn
the hair falls away from your face;
the sun turns your teeth to steel, then stone.
this takes hours.
until on the other side
you stand sweaty and petrified.
below the town lies, a dime
on its shore
that swings out
and floats among the galaxies.
this takes hours also.

THE BIOGRAPHER

Who will you find
to tell about me

but a farmer with a tricky eyelid
                in some corner of the earth

working on a wagon
with a rock chin

or travelling out to the desert
after years, a man around a fire

head a cloud
hidden in his armpit.

DEAD CHILDREN

Perhaps it is a comfort when the ancients go,
waving, leaving on clouds,
or the soldiers, finally, killed—
they rejoice, seeing the bombs come.
but even the poor love their dead children,
and take the care to wade out, dragging
                         them back by the arms,
brush the mud off; and years later
may be blowing, blowing on them,
like confused deer one sees by the highway,
circling and circling the struck young at dawn.

THE CONVERT

God's words
are cat's paws
gripping the clouds,
blasted washtubs
that speed by, or stand still

bending in the weeds
arrows fall from my ears,
the mouse in the eye of the bottle;
mad Michael stands there
holding a spear,
resplendent in tin cans
by the shivered oak.

and that is why the children
come running through the bushes
in stocking caps that are foreskins;
get caught by the hair, singing
swing up on my machines

that I unlock with a golden key,
and holding a wet finger to the air
send them with a push, on their settees,
straddling painted bombs, driving green autos,
circling and circling through the trees.

XI

PELIGROS

Ithaca House
(1971)

WAITING FOR YOU IN A COUNTRY TOWN

Across the way the lights of the old-age
                    project are dimmed:
the TVs are off, their victims prostrate
beneath gauze sheets.

starting the car I realize the trees
don't love me, neither do the cops;
they have no reason.
they beg and toss for rain,
    for another murderous hail

the depot is dark, the heart
of town; the dispatcher asleep.
I go outside and wait,
facing the time

the lines that stretch out of my
world. it comes like water
starting through a faucet, a hose growing,
and then is here, a light brighter than
                    God that
pins us to the asphalt, throws us
across buildings, speeds through the fibers
of the heart, a fist slivering.
you get off . . .

beginning again.

THINKING ON THE PLAINS

When a storm comes here
            it comes in a great bruise,
    a black prairie fire
            raging from the Llano Estacado

sheathed in dust
        everything hangs still
before the grinder,
            beneath its black ears
            and red eyes

thank God, it's no worse
        than having a tooth pulled,
in the numbness of lights
        the sound of roots tearing loose,
    of a carcass being split
        up the middle;
and just as quickly
            it's over . . .

people who love me
            don't seem to understand
    what parts I leave and what I take,
what muscle they strip
            from my bones. . . .

A HOUSE FULL OF GIRLS STRUCK BY LIGHTNING

By the time we got there
            nothing had changed

except their heat-seeking tongues
        had swelled through their teeth.

they sprawled
            where they fell,
        frozen as splinters of a pine tree
            struck down the middle

one drooped over
        the back of a chair . . .

beads in their eyes,
        their eyes gone to points,
    mouths open

their flesh still soft
            almost alive;
    there was no dust in the house.

we saw the knitting,
        the pile of dominoes,
    leaned close
        and smelled their perfume. . . .

FOR THE WEDDING NIGHT OF MATEO ESPINOZA

On their barges the Jumanos
row through the tide and the lights
before a black sea that like a storm
propels them while on the shore
chests cut by weeds and feet
stricken by vipers, the Spaniards
watch them awestruck and remember
salamanders crawling through fire,
stones that grow heads and arms
from nubs and then move. the stars
shower down on them and burn through
their armor, while years later they will find
the name of María written in the ash fluff
of those cracked breasts and shells;
                                      in her womb the
monkey glistens and scrambles for the
cold nub and the faucet, to cover
his head with a sock, his hands
with ruled paper and resin. this night,
as on all nights, the girls in Ojinaga
get down on their knees and pray
for Christmas trees, gold trees that
grow through their feet and scatter
glitter and snow bulging through
their bosoms. leaning on a fence rail
spitting out your stream of acid food
and tobacco, the same stream that we
torn through our innards drink from,
remember them and your fathers
lost in the mines with their books and chains,

their tearing doily lungs, the lust of
                    kerosene
as you lean back listening to her
belly crack and tortillas being made
with bloody thumbs, and other virgins
hopeful as Malinche wait on the shore,
cold, eyes plucked out, counting the
virtues of their spines which at times
the stars shoot down and then ignore,
and the foam crawls in to gnaw their toes. . . .

CONSEJOS

When a ghost beckons
     do not turn
 oh cowboy eating mulberries
  your boottoes on the gold
and standing on an overhanging cliff
    an angel, mist against the morning sun
 motions for you to follow
  or
camped my travellers by the
    same road, aware of someone
  throwing stones; spend the night
 huddled in the wagon
 listening to pebbles, bits of flesh
rolling from the tarp; armed
   against the night with only a shotgun
  and
chasing horses, alone
   spy a man seated on a cactus,
  fool enough to ask him
if he's seen the small bay one
and he grabbing the stirrup
   answers, teeth falling out I'll
 show you something worth far
     more than a horse,
  drag him trying to beat him off
with your whip through every bush
   and thorn, until he disgusted
lets go, lies a white thing behind
    on the ground crying Vete
 pues, ingrato, yo trataba de ayudarte. . . .

PELIGROS

Mrs. Castillo's turkeys
lunch around the back yard,
       big as oil drums

chase goats away, bite dogs, shaking
their crusted uvular fobs;
    stare at her over the stove
       through the kitchen window . . .

stand for hours on one leg, necks craned
  studying, a half mile up, vultures
     circle . . .
hummingbirds build their nests
  in the topmost branches of the elms

and at noon whirl down, pricking the eyes
  from flowers, hovering suck out the warmed
  juices with their extensile tongues

it has been reported that despite
  thick caps, padded nightshirts
maidens have been found mornings,
  their tongues gone, clawed

a strip down their back charred . . .
    the mark of a crow's foot
  across the brow, and a lump
     of gold to replace a tooth;
  after that are a complete loss

given to convulsions, babblings . . .
  in the heat of day I study the edges
  of clouds, walk country roads
    watching where hail has dropped
      study bent nails. . . .

CURSES

It travels, lightning branching
through the soil,
shoes plowing underground,
a blind snake, roots, a pig nosing
under rivers, deserts,
listening,
smelling for the blood, the
tense flower of the heart, waiting.
and when it strikes, gathering speed,
folding its tongues, leaves into a fang.
it can be in daylight,
in the middle of the night, the
victim a vessel, a husk sleeping;
it knocks him out of his life,
the bark flies, the eyes narrow,
and he runs around the house,
a mad dog before his family
howling, knocking over tables;
appears, travelling under rivers,
through cities, a cactus on a pivot.
she soothes the light
in his eyes, folds his soul
like a scarf, puts it in her pocket. . . .

HOEING ROSES

Lord, what creatures come out
black lions, jaws filth-encrusted
and waving their tentacles, shiny-horned
rhinoceros; blind wigglers
    swarming back toward damp soil

I swing my hoe to left and right
undercutting the roots, clearing the fastness
of this tangle that the former tenants
left to thrive and knot around the bushes,

grown tall and wild, but almost choked to
                ashes
in the Texas heat. still, when I turn on the
                water
at nightfall, a flower blooms into my hand,
a pellet dropped in a bowl, soft, waxen,

with the ice-thin variegation of a dawn. but
                quickly
yellows at the edges, melts back into its
                stalk; a chorus
sings, as for some santo with wooden hands
        pulled slowly, passing sad-faced
                through the streets. . . .

HISTORY OF THE BOBCAT IN NORTH AMERICA

Once he reaches the end of the branch
  this high up
        tongues sprout from his paws
   and taste the air at the end of
        the branch,
    and for the first
        time he knows what space is

behind him the hunter lies dead
    in the frozen heart of the tree,
   stiff as its phloem
 and he licking the air
      hears only the creaking of the
        snag's roots
   the echoes of his blunderbusses
        searching the slash and
        thickets,
   his hounds and gold horns
lucid snails, dried fish skeletons, leaves
        that are
       blown finally into the
           high canyons;
and behind him the hunter's heart
     hung in piñons bearded with frost
      watching
          from the forest

and lacking all resources
       but rich in dimensions
   up here so high
     the air a silver coat on his tongue
blows up his bladder
   grows silver horns;

floats out numb and half sleeping
        on his back
    circling and circling above the plateaus
and terraces,
        branching into wreckage
through the Eocene, the Cambrian
                and Pre-Cambrian. . . .

IN DEFENSE OF FROGS

Waves slip
and from the deep sea wells,
off the coal mountains
frogs swim through flowers
breaking them on their backs and eyes,
circle the ships doing backstrokes,
                              almost singing
from below attach themselves to the hull
suck with soft lips, in rhythm
lie there, slip between the ribs.
they are dancing on the decks, flopping
over the gunwales; they eat
the stores, the captain's furniture,
leave gnaw-marks on the walls
getting salt, until the masts
are gone, the wood digested
and the skeleton of the ship sinks . . .
silence. then where big and little frogs
                         float
they rise, mountains, vessels
on their heads, and holding up wire
ships, enameled ships with cunningly
contrived riggings—boats tumble
joyously up and down their arms,
three-masters pierce their stomachs—
they pass the smile around, admiring
old prizes with eyes through which
the waterlogged silver flowers pass. . . .

WALKING

Out walking one notices the homeless
dogs, those escaped from motels
jumped from tourists' windows,
pushed from cars, kicked out of houses,
abandoned surreptitiously at midnight
by laughing couples travelling through.
those not killed by wolves, by lack
of water, porcupines, empaled on
thorns, mornings creep into town.
rummage about the courthouse, the
city jail, outside the school; try to
                    barge in
from the cold. race through ballgames,
after try to follow boys home. their
pee freezes yellow on cornerstones.
out walking they eye me from bushes,
gallop over, growing thin, eyes fading;
love streams from their mouths . . .

on slack afternoons the sheriff's
deputy, for nothing to do takes his
shotgun and cruises about town; executes
them on the city dump. or a flood
catches them sleeping in the arroyo,
carries them howling through town.
at night crouched outside boys' houses
alert, waiting to be called. or too
weak to catch rats, diseased
make a last sacrifice of themselves
the best they know how, lying
on their backs frozen, their
bloody paws held up to the moon. . . .

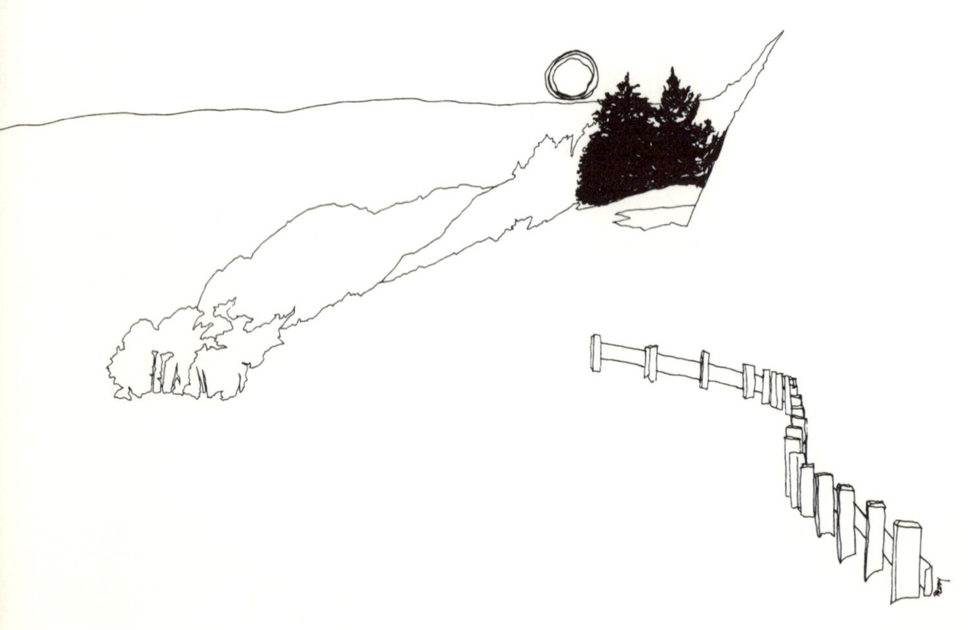

XII

NEW POEMS

THE BAT

We put him in the old white bird cage
where the spaces were too big—
but he stayed
to catch at our fingers with his claws,
leaning forward with his Devil's head
to eat our white bread.

FRENETIC MAN FLYING BY ON A CLOUD

First there is a distant tower
of smoke, a flailing of arms
as from angry Hindu gods, steam
from a golden nose, a
thundersome platform moving
toward us like a storm; white
sparks fly through clouds, the
ground rolls, men choke. and
soon he is shooting over at the
level of the eucalypti, divested;
chickens fall down wells, bark
curls from trees. he shakes
off his pearls, his leather jacket
from his shoulders, drops his beads;
and picking up speed sails arms
folded through the shreds of his own
letters, complacent, looking straight
ahead, pulling on his hookah toward
other rivers, other cities. . . .

GOING DOWN THE BLUE CREEK TRAIL
for Bill

You are a two-headed clown
        waddling in front of me,
    holes running up your ribs,
        your straw hat blasted apart
            showing the scarf, your red brains.
you turn and flash your gold teeth.
    this is a time to be funny. and fade
into the cluster of insects that love you,
                making a great brown flower.
our eyes drip no water,
            but blood,
    we are swimming through the pines
  and the ciénaga grass up to our chins.
you start barking.
and appear again on the other side of the meadow
        in robes, silent, walking slowly
    with a thin belled weed that tears through the clouds,
            altar boy
                in curls
                exorcising the world.

THE TOUR

Suddenly it is dangerous
where he has been

a world tilted
by cataclysm.

behind him his gruel shadow,
a trail of corn. that swings

through his feet, a tongue
pointing forward

a path
leading among the stars.

TALKING WITH THE COOK WHEN
THE FIRST MAN COMES TO COFFEE

In the sky
gauze patches
soak over our wounds
that drip sparks,
flying in a second to the horizon.

we dig our needle
heels in against it, our spurs
founder in the dust
up to our knees. the calf
gone mad on his white
intestine of a rope.

until the first hand
closes around the cup,
a scar covered with hair
and the light shines out
            from the tips of our boots.

THE RABBITS

The things have all run off
into the salt thickets, which
around here are known as
No Man's Land, because they go on
at least to Cow Heaven.

and have, here and there,
only an old cowboy's shack
where the raccoons on hard days visit
and maybe an oil pump
withered against the landscape.

after a windstorm the alkali
coats the branches and your face, like snow,
yes a type of aesthetics, and you know
they are down there hunched in the brakes
with the rattlesnakes in the swamps that somewhere
       become a river

because at night getting brave or maybe scared
lying on your belly you can hear them talking,
a syllable of your name, dice clicking,
and mornings catch a glimpse of clouds near in the bushes,
their small teeth dripping fire

a curl of smoke in the eye, but
disappear as you reach for your gun,
shuffling off whispering Ave, Ave,
biting their beads, and leaving
strange footprints in the sand.

CONCERT

The old people come
and sit on the grass
or in chairs they bring.
up front a few children
frolic making faces
at the trombones warming up,
then they sit down, too.
the American Legion Band
plays the Tennessee Waltz
and something sweet from Mendelssohn.
the clarinet squeaks.
into a silvery fog
the red sun is dissolving. slowly
everyone gets up and leaves
as night comes flooding in under the maples,
and behind them in the dark
as cars start, head home,
balloons bob and settle, paper bags
glow beneath the trees. . . .

CLOUD FOREST

Below our feet the slope to the sea
            granite cobbles steaming in the heat
                        black mesquite
but here the clouds come nosing in
            every afternoon, pigs through the trees.
it goes dark with their white.
        as pans rattle in the kitchen we listen to the dripping,
    and go to sleep, blood falling on the tin roof.
mornings everything tears before our boots;
        we go in more than couples,
                    stick to the paths;
the warning: caverns hollowed out by streams
        the livestock falls through.
across your face a fern
    dangles out of a tree like a noose.
off the trail somewhere a goat bleats. . . .

WETBACK

Down in Big Nations Canyon
past the Boy Scout camp on the plains at its mouth
and the forest of totems,
where you sink to the hips in sand
scrambling upstream against the current,
and having your lunch by a pool the donkeys
come stampeding to beg an apple,
steal a sandwich, then run off
to look back, eyes crossed from the thorns.
past all that, watching a tarantula fighting the cold
wandering drunken—
past where it would take weeks to travel
if there were enough sun—
we came upon the ruins of a wetback's fire,
neat, star-shaped,
a drop of blood on the ground
and plunging our hands in to the wrists
finding them cold turned and went back home;
and while they were playing salutes, we
filling the house with candles as the sky
with its clouds and planets rushed
streaked and mad over, he was running
through the piled driftwood of the mountains
breaking his legs in cracks, the tongue
a round saw cutting a hole in his head, parts
of his flesh eaten raw to the bone. . . .

BURRO MESA

Walking across the blessed crewcut skull
up the old Model A road
now staked we are not looking for peaks
because there are none, but convolutions.
we scratch your ears, beneath our feet a purr.

and in and out the yucca and grass hills
where the farmer drove mad with circles and the
sun, his wife, doves coo
the eyes and legs tangled—
yet there is one on the far edge,
a layered red thumb, and all around
the washes and skunks, still cracking.

up here there is no one
though it is Easter and we have our
hats on, we came steeled,
prepared. though at the stone corral
large as a football field and square
where above the Indians fell slow
as possible down the cliffs
before the astounded ranch house—
in its guts we find a Coors can.

and fly over the pour off
unlacing our boots,
into the canyon, nut trees,
out of the wind, and back into the bowl
all dark, where above the sun shines
through the red cliffs, like flesh.
eat our lunch hands dead in the boulders
beneath a hummingbird

and climbing out shot
in the knees and plexus,
expecting strangely to live, across
the flood plain breaking the scattered teeth
born from the rock and goat bone chips,
storm through the cat claw and tules
toward the shadow, tearing our skin, not caring
where we step. the cornered pigs
flash their fangs and dash off. we
drink the water from their hoofprints.

THE CALL

When you called we were napping
and rose that Saturday afternoon, ghosts
from our secrets,
to your voice, dim on the phone
but laughing, telling us how
months ago you had almost drowned,
blacking out and sinking to the bottom of the pool.
I saw your long body twisting as in love,
myself struck to the lungs,
going down to the center of the dream, sprawling,
the hair spread out, settling around you,
the sharp bubbles trailing from your nose,
and then lie still
in the puddle of your blood
as your arms folded
and your nipples crept out
becoming their final silver
to taste the cold. beneath the same sky
that is above us, falling
into yourself as we breathed, and your voice
months ago, laughing over the bad lines
from Los Angeles, speaking to us
out of the phone, as if through water. . . .

THE SEASON

At night a few spears of fire
shoot from the horizon.
the coyotes come in to rummage through the trash cans
and paper bags blown against the old fence.
you listen to the wagons rumble by
bearing away the dead, sitting upright.
you keep your books packed,
the shotgun loaded under the bed.
you can hardly speak in sentences.

DISTANCES

This is what distance is
after lunch,
driving west from Las Cruces
fifty miles of evil, the little car
breasting the sage.
after cokes and gas to Lordsburg
the same, the heat in our armpits.
in the setting sun the mountains
running ahead of us
waving their arms, as did Pancho Villa.
we stand on the balcony
as the wind uncurls from our throats
and measure the size of the town
against a train snaking through,
against the brown sweep to the mountains,
creased and setting their claws.
below the streets close,
beside the plastic awnings
of the next motel a girl
legs through the mercury pool.
the lights are coming on;
my head still spins.
and go in from the quiet to our room
                          with its conveniences;
climb a stool in the bathroom to watch
the red sun burn a peak through, a dirty woman
in her back yard making tortillas. sit legs up
in front of a film about beavers.

THE CAMPER

Like words
his footprints go before him
over the gravel, over the cracks between boulders,
into the dark crevices of heat.
the dun eagles swoop on updrafts
back and forth between the rainbow cliffs.
by daylight the skunks are rabid;
he follows his stick with the head of an adder,
losing chests and bolls of his flesh, a sheep through cactus
until at the crack, powder, rocks shattered, where
smugglers' burros dance, candles
up and down the cliffs, and at the bottom
a grove and the river, plunges in;
makes his camp, a star spread on the sand.
and lying by it, iron in a blanket
the heat bubbles from the top of his head
as an owl skips over driftwood after fish, and
the spindly wild dogs come up to lick his ears.

FOR JUDY JUKOWSKI

In Lincoln it is cold tonight
and over the plains in between where the snow
grows like moss among the stubble
the California condor sweeps
without tipping its wings,
from Montana to Florida.
ash drips from his lizard teeth.
your voice is a worm
          working at the top of my jawbone.
after, my dog dances around the house
like Priscilla's dog over her report card;
the list slides into an envelope,
the fingerbones you requested.
I put the old confetti ribbons on that make make my legs green.
but then she is in my arms with her arms around my neck
and won't let go; I must look into those buck eyes.
I must carry her off to bed.
I find myself way past midnight
when even cocks are asleep
rummaging among the camping gear,
cleaning the excellent knife, like
a miner finding himself at daylight
scraping pans at the edges of a nameless
stream.

THE CHISHOLM TRAIL

Out of the gray grass
like a canvas the cattle
nearing at the tip of the infinite line
shy from us, dodge from our camera.

a cowboy in his wooly chaps
has come riding up and
under the black shadow of his broad hat
smiles

in this heat that is more than a dust
buttes, the sky from its horizon has separated
as the hair lifts from our scalps.
around our feet the toes shoot out soft jets
                                 of feathers and flame.

the earth chokes white in a wave. his
pistols grow large, pearl iridaceous;
one cow comes up but her arm falls off
boiled when she reaches to touch us on the face.

FAROS

Traveller all Spanish blood
a steel-mesh ship burning in the harbor
going backwards and forward.
out on its cardboard rock the little one shoots
            its blessings of square machinegun bullets.
but there are no women behind you,
    only a good meal, your tie, two pressed tongues
and the smell of your coat.
you tug at your rainhat
                with your thumb,
eyes painted on.
and here is another at your elbow,
    substantial, up high red and glowing.
the door is only two inches tall
            but you make a note and then step in.

SIERRA BLANCA

If an eagle
should fall,
a drop of lead paint

smashing houses on pilings
smashing over rocks,
and we standing here see

an arrow piercing a clock
as below the plain goes out
under its bath of heat

then rises
to where we are
and beyond, a mist, a space.

below the town lies
with broken arms among its boulders
boards and urine

its celebration
the Texaco station
while behind

the wind thunders in our ear roots
up on the ledges lion cubs
squall in the sun

where no man is.

CROSSING A PLATEAU

174

Out here the highways go on and on
you can drive all day and never meet a car
                              and if you do
you stumble out, embrace, exchange family pictures

standing in a bowl
the edges tilt up, lost
across the middle of yourself;
and always ahead, a hint of peaks and waves,
                    the liquid lie of mountains
          which you know, getting there, are scars and rifts
                              formed drip by drip,
                         as if it will take you
                         that long.

ON THE BORDER WITH CROOK

You climb up hills.
firing your carbine.
you are both thirsty and cold
at the same time.

every morning vistas open;
damsels who cut their
legs. on the peaks lightnings,
mountains groaning in their shrouds.
you give them Roman names

while before his visage,
distant, on the clouds, leading.
this is why you oil your pistols,
the voice of a senator

until they come, bloodied string
out of the brakes, dragged at the ends
of their horses; in your blouse you hide
the relic of Tall Wolf, necklace
of human fingers,

flour, corn, and spades.
and seated before you, Crazy Horse
and Spotted Tail, see the ghosts
dying over their stares, as they begin
to dance, welcome or not, across your eyes.